The X Stands for Excellence

Based on the Seven Ups of Life Presentation

Alfonzo Porter
Silver Tip Productions

Copyright © 1996 by Alfonzo Porter

ISBN 0-7872-2358-1

All rights reserved. No part of this publication may be reproduced, stored in a retrieval system, or transmitted, in any form or by any means, electronic, mechanical, photocopying, recording, or otherwise, without the prior written permission of the copyright owner.

Printed in the United States of America

10 9 8 7 6 5 4 3 2 1

CONTENTS

Foreword *vii*
Acknowledgments *ix*
Introduction *xiii*

✗ *Chapter One*

Wake Up 3

Self-Esteem 5
Fear 8
Change 9
Conception 10
Education 10
Equity 11

✗ *Chapter Two*

Rise Up 17

The Crisis of Youth 17
Morality vs. Entertainment 19
Adultism 20
Power 22

✗ *Chapter Three*

Listen Up 25

It Ain't My Fault 25
Bad News 26

X Generation 28
Musical Messages 29
Finding Your Power 30

✗ *Chapter Four*

Hurry Up 33

Doing For Others 34
Ameri-Corp Program 34
Real Life Hero—C.D. Banks 36
Lawsuit Mania 37

✗ *Chapter Five*

Cheer Up 41

Short-Term Goals 42
Take Action 43
I Can Do That!! 43
Goals 46

✗ *Chapter Six*

Look Up 49

Fourth Grade Blues 49
Five Times as Much 50
Ten Commandments of Success 52
What Is Success? 53
Belief 54

✗ *Chapter Seven*
Never Give Up 57
Hate Groups 58
Grades of Humanity 58
Home Talk 59
Blatant Hypocrisy 60
Showing Them How 61
What Do We Want? 61
Passing the Baton 63
The Code of Perseverance 65

References 67

FOREWORD

Al Porter's new book, *The X Stands for Excellence,* is a fresh approach to the best standard. Excellent comes from the Greek word "kello," meaning to impel, or "celsus" to raise high. In Latin the "excello" means to surpass in good qualities or deeds. In teen-talk "to out-do"; or in street slang talk "to slam or to jam."

In our world today where "put-downs" are the word games we play in and out of the school yard, "pick-me-up's" are very seldom used; knowing how to "rap" seems more important than having your life on a "map"; where playing "b-ball" and hangin' in the halls or at the mall is more important than where one can start college in the fall; where dope has taken hope; where "whatz-up" is having babies and your life filled with "maybe's" or I wish I should've, could've, would've done that, been that, but not now.

In these downward-bound times we need some "ups" and *The X Stands for Excellence* is a powerful upper. It deals with unity in a multi-cultural society. It creates a spark to wake-up your talents. It makes things happen by rising-up, instead of drying-up. It gives a sense of confidence as you listen-up, promotes self-esteem as you hurry-up to cheer-up as you look-up—and asks you to hear your voice within that says, never give-up.

Congratulations Al Porter for this extra-mile highway of knowledge.

—Harvey Alston
C.E.O., Best, Inc.

–ACKNOWLEDGMENTS–

I would like to first acknowledge Edream Porter, my mother, for being the best mother in the world! Understanding, patient, wise, hardworking, humble, elegant and loving are but a few adjectives I use to describe her. She single-handedly raised six children while working a full-time job and pursuing a high school GED at night. We never had a lot of material things, but we did have a loving family who supported and encouraged each other. She provided an environment of warmth and safety in the midst of violence and chaos right outside our door. She struggled to make men of five boys without a father figure. And, she did a great job! As a result of her struggles and positive example, we work hard, don't break the law, and are good parents.

Born in Cotton Plant, Arkansas, during the Depression, she learned early that being the daughter of a sharecropper was not going to be an easy life. She began at the age of five chopping and picking cotton in Matthews, Missouri, where her father had re-located when she was three.

By the time she started going to school at the age of seven, she had already worked full-time for two years. The school house consisted of one classroom and one teacher. When she turned eight, her father re-located again, this time to Portageville, Missouri. She was forced to drop out of school at the age of eight because the town did not have a school for blacks. It would take two years before the school board would finally decide to open a two room house as a school for blacks.

Sharecropping was one step above slavery and not a big step. Working for a gentleman by the name of Theodore Brand, my grandfather's crops would always somehow just barely meet the tally. That meant no money for working in the fields all season. My grandfather would later work for a man by the name of Voss. His philosophy espoused to all the blacks who worked for him was, "eating ain't nothing but a habit."

Education continued to be sporadic because of the need for help in the fields. She was never encouraged by her father to seek independence and was told that she would never make it on her own by members of the family.

She met Esther Clark and had two sons, my brothers John and Aaron. They were never married. He died an alcoholic in 1958. She then met my father, Henry Duncan, in 1959 and had four children. She left him in 1965 to move to St. Louis, Missouri, in search of greater opportunities.

We moved into the Darst-Webbe housing project in 1965 and lived there until 1974. During that time she worked full-time in the cafeteria of the Mental Hospital across the street, while also going to school to finish a high school GED.

She provided such an image of strength and determination that we all learned and benefited from. Thanks for everything you did and for all that you tried to do but couldn't. Although I, at times, did not express our appreciation for your efforts, in retrospect, I can say that we were all blessed to have had you as a mother.

Thanks to my brother Richard for his honest outlook on life. It reminds me of the line from Hamlet, where the father, Pololnius, said to his son, "to thine own self be true." He always had a strong sense of himself. He didn't take crap from people and was never accused of holding his tongue. We all need a little bit of honesty in our lives.

To my brother Willie for his style and pride. When it comes to dressing up, he's the heavyweight champion. Also, for the strength that he has shown throughout many difficult times in his life. Despite it all, he exudes confidence and self pride.

To Aaron for his mastery for building something out of nothing. I was able to use that knowledge to build my own bicycles from scratch because I could not afford a new one. He also was the first to show me that the world extended beyond the neighborhood where we grew up.

To my late brother John who was thrust into the difficult position of guardian. I didn't like the authority he exercised over me, but, in retrospect, I thank God for him!

To my one and only sister, Morney, for demonstrating strength and ability in everything she did. I know she wanted to kill each and every one of us at some point; maybe all at the same time. No matter what the task, she seemed to be able to handle it and do well.

Thank you to all the young people in schools and organizations all across America for making me feel welcome and accepted.

To Harvey Alston for providing the guidance and direction I needed in order to do many of the things I have done over the past five years. I have gained recognition as a professional speaker, traveled around the country, grown immensely as a person, focused sharply upon my vision, wrote a book, and gained a great and true friend.

To my good friend Christopher Durham for trying to keep me sane. It didn't work!

To Maggie Burns and Tom Barfield for being there in times of great need.

Thanks to the best co-workers in the world with the JCG program. You are caring, insightful, and all beautiful people. You make working a pleasure.

Thanks to Mike Frank, Dwight Loken and Kelly Hillier for providing an opportunity for me to move forward as a professional speaker.

—INTRODUCTION—

Childhood in America has become a treacherous rite of passage. Nearly one million cases of child abuse, neglect, and and sexual and emotional assaults were filed last year. While crime in the general population has decreased over the past three years, juvenile crime continues to skyrocket. Gangs have extended their reach all across the country and are recruiting directly from many of our public schools. If kids can survive their childhood in America, they may stand a chance at only being borderline dysfunctional.

As our society searches for the reasons and possible solutions to the issues of violence, crime, poverty, and abuse, we as adults, parents, and teachers cannot hope to escape the blame. Because of this neglectful attitude towards our children, some are even asking whether America will survive?

Many have already given up on this generation of youth, dubbing them Generation X. But many of us know better! I can point you to several reasons to be optimistic. Hundreds of thousands of young people across America are involved in positive programs like the Ameri-Corp program, the Hugh O'Brien programs, Teen Institute, Ohio Business Week, Future Homemakers of America (FHA), Distributive Education Clubs of America (DECA), Business Professionals of America (BPA), Future Business Leaders of America (FBLA), Jobs for America's Graduates (JAG), and Project Academic Excellence, to name a very few. If you have ever been to any of these programs and witnessed the absolute electricity among the participants, you too would be optimistic. The trouble is that you never hear about them because our newspapers and television stations focus primarily on the negatives.

This book is meant to point out the mistakes we adults have made, as well as to suggest a few common sense and practical solutions in working with teens today.

Because I grew up in a difficult environment, I understand how low expectations can really hurt one's outlook for the future. One's mother or father's occupation and earning potential should not be a determining factor in what knowledge they may be exposed to in school.

I work today with high school seniors from what many call the hardest neighborhood in our city. I have met some of the nicest, most articulate, bright, and spiritual young people I have ever worked with. I believe that they can all be successful. The problem is, they don't believe it. Many of them fall victim of the same face saving lies we all learn to tell. Give a straight face and say with conviction that you are going to college. Never mind the fact that your cumulative grade point average is 1.250, you've missed one-fourth of the days in school, you have no way to pay for school, and that you really don't want to go any way.

The hard reality is that socio-economics is one of the main determinants for gaining access to success. One's environment should have little to do with educational opportunities. Determination, perseverance, vision, and action are the ingredients our young people need. Let's build them up instead of tearing them down.

Jesse Jackson came to my little ghetto high school in St. Louis and told me to proclaim that, "I am Somebody!!" It was the first time that I had ever said anything so positive about myself out loud. It was a tremendous boost to my self image. I often times think back to how that made me feel. I felt so good, I'm sure I levitated out of the auditorium. We've got to find that kind of inspiration for teens today. It will take a concerted, organized effort. But it can and must be done!

The X Stands for Excellence

Wake Up

We can no longer afford "throw away" children. We need them all! Provide equal educational opportunities with similar expectations for achievement and success. Technology in schools should be accessible to every child regardless of where they live or the socio-economic status of their family.

Al Porter

Chapter One

Wake Up

Growing up, I had a blind trust in adults that disappeared somewhere in my early teens. It was the kind of trust that made me believe that all adults were on my side, and that no adult would lie to me or try to abuse me for their own purposes. Most American kids are raised that way. What is most amazing is that I grew up with those kinds of beliefs even though the environment was nearly devoid of hope, and it was common knowledge that not just a few of the adults in the community were capable of harming us and often times relished the opportunity to do so. The Darst-Webbe housing projects, where I spent many of my formative years, was both horrible and fantastic at the same time. Many of the things that happened and that my sisters and brothers witnessed were never seen on "Leave It To Beaver," or any of the other programs that painted such a wonderful picture of American life.

Ward Cleaver never came home and slapped June upside the head because he was drunk and his dinner wasn't ready. Wally didn't get anybody pregnant. The Beave wasn't in a gang. The family never had any loud arguments where they would throw things at one another. They never had any money problems. The neighborhood was always spotless and everyone was usually polite and courteous.

On The Brady Bunch, Mike Brady was not having an incestuous relationship with Marcia, Jan or Cindy. Alice, the housekeeper, didn't secretly abuse the kids while the Brady's were out on the town, and Greg didn't have a heroin problem. This was almost in complete contrast with my reality. Many of these things did not happen in my household, but they were all around us. We knew people who were the victims of nearly every evil imaginable. I believed that my life should be a mirror image of the Cleavers and the Bradys and because it wasn't, I suffered tremendous self-doubt and a low self-image.

I also believed the information presented in school painted an accurate picture of the world and the way it functioned. I was learning and reciting the Pledge of Allegiance while African Americans were still being denied basic rights in the South. I was required to sing the Star Spangled Banner every morning at the beginning of school. We were singing about independence and freedom, but the words meant nothing to me. How could we sing such songs and recite such words when, in fact, they were not true for tens of millions of Americans? Asking that question in school in those days would draw a stern look of disapproval from the teacher. I quickly learned to "go along to get along." If I wanted to be successful, I couldn't ask difficult questions. But doesn't that defeat the entire purpose of education? I didn't learn what I wanted to know at all. I learned what someone else wanted to teach me. Lulled into pacifism, I became convinced that all I had to do was to stay out of trouble, respect my elders, and do well in school and everything would be fine. That too turned out to be a lie.

We must realize that painting a perfect picture and passing it off as the reality of life, or some standard to be upheld by everyone is unrealistic. It causes many of us to accept things as fact when they are based in fiction.

We have passed on this fantastic idea that our society has been this great place. The curriculum in our public schools bear, at least, some of the responsibility for this misinformation. In fact, it has not been a kind place for women, children, or minorities. Historically, we have been treated with a great deal of disdain, scorn, and contempt.

The truth is that violence and abuse were once a normal part of maintaining family order. Traditional Anglo-American law allowed a man to "discipline" his wife with corporal punishment. Women were, in essence, the property of the man. She could not assert any rights or privileges above his. Her role was simply to have his children, raise them, and make sure that his home was kept. Speaking out of turn or questioning a decision could be dangerous. In some places, disobedience from a child was seen as a small form of treason, punishable, at least in theory, by death.

The thirteenth amendment abolished the slavery of African Americans as well as involuntary servitude and took away the man's "kingly" powers. Many members of congress refused to vote for the bill until they were assured that it would not allow wives to escape the husband's dominance in the family.

Despite chilling examples of over-disciplining our mothers and children, our society started organizations against cruelty to animals many years before we even thought to form a society which would grant equal protection to children.

We have also been a nation that has fostered outrageous ideas against blacks and people of color. We were told that we were less than human and incapable of learning. It was against the law to try to teach us. We were looked upon and treated like poor, pitiful, and pathetic creatures not deserving respect, dignity, or pride. We were sold at public auction as if we were things instead of people. After the 13th Amendment, we were terrorized by viscous hate groups and relegated to second class citizenship. We could not vote because of Poll Taxes and Grandfather Clauses. Dogs were sicked on us, and firehoses were turned on us in the 1960's simply for asking for the rights guaranteed in the Constitution in 1776. While gleefully singing the National Anthem, and reciting the Pledge of Allegiance and the Declaration of Independence we still wait for the rights of almost 200 years ago.

Even as a child I knew that this was hypocritical and false. We must be more truthful and inclusive in our school curriculums and life lessons if we reasonably expect all young people to have high levels of self-esteem.

Self-Esteem

As babies we are always told how cute and adorable we are. We are the apple of everyone's eye and the center of attention. I don't know about you, but I really liked that. What happened to it?

Self-esteem is defined as how we perceive ourselves physically, mentally, and emotionally. Self-esteem also means how we feel about our race or ethnic group.

We are influenced by things outside of ourselves, which includes situations, circumstances, people, and things. We are constantly seeking the approval of others. Our thinking and behavior is always in anticipation of a response. It is, therefore, based in fear. We are afraid of being rejected by our peer group or having little control or power to regulate these things.

Our ego creates our self image. However, our ego is not really who we are. It is our social mask. It is the role we play in life. This social mask thrives on approval. It wants to control. It is sustained by power, because it lives in fear. We are afraid of things that cannot hurt us. And, this is, perhaps, the largest barrier to many of us feeling good about who we really are.

Teens Can Improve Self-Esteem by:

✗ Taking action on those things that you really believe in.

✗ Writing down all of your accomplishments.

✗ Identifying your strengths.

✗ Exercising regularly.

✗ Reading positive and encouraging literature.

Fear

Motivational speaker Les Brown said that when he was young he'd have to walk to school. Every day, he would encounter a neighborhood dog that would chase him for blocks. This went on for quite some time until, finally, Les declared that he had it with this bully mongrel. He decided that he would stand tall and confront the dog. He was absolutely terrified of this hound but was resolute in his determination not to give in to his fear. Then the fateful day came. He was confronted face-to-face with his nemesis. He turned around, looked the dog right in the face and said, "Come on, I'm not running from you any more. Come on!" But as the dog approached, Les noticed something very strange about it. The dog had no teeth!

He spent many months living in fear of something that could not harm him. He uses the acronyms for FEAR to mean "false evidences appearing real." That is, we believe that we can be hurt by things that have no power or control over our self. We grant that power to other people, our peer groups, teachers, parents, situations, and circumstances. We hope for their approval and acceptance and when we don't get it, our self-esteem is damaged. We can improve our self-esteem by realizing that our true selves, that is who we really are, our spirit, our souls, are completely free of those things. We are immune to criticism. It is unfearful of any challenge, and it falls beneath no one. Yet, we can also be humble and feel superior to no one because we will realize that everyone is the same. Because we are all human, we have the same kinds of fears.

By verbalizing and thinking in terms of the positives, our subconscious will affect our conscious mind causing us to act positively instead of reacting to what others do or feel. However, the way we feel about ourselves may also be enhanced when you receive positive feedback from others and when you feel connected and are helping or caring for others. We have such great potential among the youth of this nation. The feedback adults give to them is typically negative and mostly untrue. There must be a change in the basic way that adults perceive youth and teens.

Change

Rip Van Winkle was a nice kindly old gentleman living in up state New York in the mid-1750's. He became famous to many of us in elementary school as the man who slept for 20 years, but part of the story was left out. Rip had a very domineering wife who would complain incessantly about all of Rip's shortcomings as a provider and spouse. She complained so much that Rip would leave the house everyday to take a walk to escape his home situation and have time for private meditation. One day, Rip encountered a gentleman who was delivering liquor to the local saloons and asked Rip if he might give him a hand. They unloaded the stock over a period of hours. Unbeknownst to the delivery driver, Rip was secretly taking a sampling of all the brands of liquor. And before the two men were finished with the job, Rip was bombed! He walked around for hours trying to find his house, but couldn't. He finally gave up and found a tree that he could lean against and get some rest. He quickly fell into a deep, coma-like sleep.

When Rip Van Winkle went to sleep, there was a picture of King George III on his wall at home. When he woke up 20 years later, there was a picture of George Washington hanging in its place. By the time Rip Van Winkle woke up, the whole world had changed. The world is in a constant state of change. Just like in Rip Van Winkle's day, it is as apparent as ever.

For example, 20 years ago, America was the producer, manufacturer and provider of nearly any good or product on the market. Twenty years later, we find that our economic opportunities for the future are tied to the merger with Mexico and Canada. We need the 55 million or so citizens of Canada and the 70 million citizens of Mexico to buy and consume what products America still produces in order to sustain our standard of living. America used to produce the best of everything with little substantial competition from anyone. Our cars were superior; they are not anymore. Our computer and office equipment was the best in the world; this is no longer true. Production of electronic equipment such as televisions, stereo systems, speakers, and radios was dominated by the U.S.; today, it is difficult to find an American made television set. Through our textile industry, we clothed the world. However, most of the clothing that I purchase today is not made in America. I actively inspect the labels, but if I only wore what is made in America, either I'd be drastically out of style or naked.

Much like Rip Van Winkle, we have awakened, and the whole world has changed. This fact has prompted the question; where will the jobs in the future come from? How will today's young people find meaningful work as we move into the new millennium? How will they jettison into a new age of cyberspace when they are studying from twenty five year old textbooks? How can they conceive the level to which they must elevate without us fully doing our part? We must make sure that all school children in America have access to the latest technology.

Conception

My favorite cartoon growing up was *The Jetsons*. I still can't wait for the day when my car can fly, I can get a robot as a maid, work a grueling 3 hours a day, live in a Sky Pad apartment, and hear my dog talk!

At the rate things are changing, it won't be long now. I have always been told that, "if your mind can conceive it, your heart believe it, you can achieve it." Rip Van Winkle never imagined airplanes, computers, space shuttles, and World Wide Webs.

Can we really say that, within the next ten years, we won't encounter some other forms of life as we continue to uncover new planets and solar systems?

I jokingly talk about the day we encounter Klingons, Romulans, Bejorins, Ferengi, and Vulcans. But whose to say that we won't in this new age? Technology is moving exponentially and we have little clue as to what really lies ahead. It's funny that on the day we do discover life from other planets, our problems between black, white, brown, red, and yellow will seem completely insignificant. Can you conceive it?

Conception means very little, in my opinion, without education. One could conceive great things, but with no idea or set methods as to how to accomplish a task, the conception seems irrelevant.

Education

Our economy has moved from manufacturing goods to providing services. Many of these services will be technical in nature. This means that a good education will become even more important to the success of young people. A person could be in school for the rest of their life because of the rate at which technology has and is moving. The knowledge gained through receiving a degree in computer science in 1995 will be of almost no use in the year 2000 if the knowledge base is not constantly upgraded. Continuing education will not only be encouraged by corporate America, but it will be required. In many fields, this has been true for years.

Teachers must maintain certification. Lawyers are required by the Bar Association to keep abreast of case precedent. Doctors need to know the latest surgical procedures or about new medications and treatments. Many of us would probably shake with fear if we thought doctors, lawyers, and the engineers who build bridges, skyscrapers, and roadways were not kept to a certain standard of education and re-training. Those expectations of more schooling are common place in many companies even today. Teens must recognize that continuing education will be a part of their success. Resign yourself to the fact that you will be school for the rest of your life.

Without continuing training, we might wake up one day and, much like Rip Van Winkle, discover that we are in a totally new and different world incapable of making sense of the rapid changes.

Equity

These new changes will demand that every child in our society has an opportunity for an education equal in quality. Many kids who attend schools in middle to upper middle class suburban areas or wealthier neighborhoods believe that, for the most part, all schools are basically like theirs. That there are enough textbooks, supplies, materials, and equipment to go around. This assumption is misleading. In America we have children who attend schools that are in such conditions of dis-repair that the buildings should be condemned. Books are scarce, supplies and equipment virtually non-existent, and teachers horribly frustrated by the lack of tools necessary to be effective in delivering quality instruction.

An excellent case would be the city not far from my home town of St. Louis, Missouri. The City of East St. Louis, Illinois, sits across the Mississippi River from the gleaming Gateway Arch and the skyscrapers of St. Louis.

If a person can go to school in East St. Louis, graduate, go to college, and make a success of his or her life, then they deserve a medal!

The City of East St. Louis has no sewer control and no garbage pick up. The residents burn their trash in vacant lots to get rid of it. This has caused a problem with rats, which have been estimated to be the size of small dogs. The local paper reported that the soil in the entire city is contaminated with lead poisoning from plants spewing toxic chemicals into the air. And even though the plants operate in East St. Louis, they pay no taxes to support the city or the school district. Plants like Big River Zinc, Cerro Copper ("America's Largest Recycler of Copper," according to the sign), and the Monsanto chemical plant are a few.

Though East St. Louis is the largest city south of Springfield, and has a population in excess of 30,000 people, it has been left off the Illinois map. Crime has reached dizzying proportions, largely due to the lack of police protection. There is no hospital or clinic in the city to deliver a baby. It has some of the sickest children in the country. The school system has about 16,000 students. Every academic program offered by the school system has been stripped to the bone and beyond, except music and sports. Some classes go without a teacher because the district cannot afford to pay for substitutes. There is no technology in the schools. The latest equipment available to students are electric typewriters from the 1950's. Academics like chemistry are estimated to be 30-50 years behind.

The problems of the city pour right through the doors of the schools. A junior high school was evacuated after sewage flowed into the kitchen. Two days later one of the city's high schools was overflown with raw waste for the second time that year. The school had to be closed because of the fumes of backed-up toilets. Sewage flowed through the floor, then turned up in the kitchen and the student's bathroom.

That same week the district announced the lay-offs of 280 teachers, 166 cooks and cafeteria workers, 25 teacher aides, and 34 custodians, painters, electricians and building engineers. There is very little hope for anyone who lives in the city and attends the schools. But much to their credit and praise, many students in this desperate environment remain hopeful that the situation will improve.

A few years ago while visiting my family in St. Louis, I read an article in the *St. Louis Post-Dispatch* which was a compilation of interviews with graduates of East St. Louis schools. Many were in college and doing well. Some had graduated from college and were promising to return to their city and help re-build. There is a sense of belief in many of the young people who go to school in East St. Louis. A few of the graduates are now personal friends of mine. Listening to them describe the conditions under which they went to school, many questions are raised about the level of fairness and equality in our school systems.

Is it realistic for us to expect all American youth to feel good about themselves regardless of their circumstances? Do we also believe that we can ever hope to solve many of our social problems when so many who are not provided with the basic necessities? Wake Up!!

The top one percent of the population has as much income as the bottom 50 percent. The gap between the rich and the poor has widened and the gap between the rich and the middle class has also grown in 46 states since the mid 1980's.

In her article entitled, "Social Class and School Knowledge," Jean Anyon said that social and economic class determined what knowledge a person was exposed to. She identified four specific classes and outlined the expectations for the students. The first type of school is the working class school. In this school, the fathers, if they were around, were unskilled or semi-skilled workers. Some in this group lived below poverty level but most were above, though slightly. The next group were the *middle class schools*. In these schools, the kids were from homes where the parents were public school teachers, social workers, accountants, and middle managers in corporations. Then there was the *affluent professional school* where parents were highly paid doctors, television personalities, high level executives and university professors. Finally, there was the *executive elite school*. These schools accepted the children of corporate vice presidents, CEO's, and politicians. Their incomes rate in the top two percent.

What is interesting is that each of the schools had a theme that was dominant to only that particular income/economic group. For instance, in the *working class school*, the theme is resistance to education. This is characterized by the resistance on the part of the students to the learning process. The students are seen as apathetic and uninterested in what the teacher does, regardless as to what it happens to be. More often, heads would be on desks during class, there is no enthusiasm, and the students often pay absolutely no attention to what the teachers is saying. The children learned fragmented facts which could not really be connected to larger bodies of knowledge. Sustained academic knowledge has only an occasional presence in the *working class school.*

The theme in the *middle class school* is that of possibility. It is possible for the students to do or go wherever they want to in life. They are provided with a sense of preparing for higher education. The curriculum is made flexible and methods of teaching and administering the learning process revolve around student needs. There is an emphasis on patriotism in the *middle class school* more so than in the other income levels.

In the *affluent professional school,* the theme is what Anyon calls narcissism. In other words, individualism. There is an emphasis on thinking for oneself, on externalizing, on peìßonal development, and creativity. There is also some emphasis on humanitarianism; doing something for someone else. But giving is characterized by financial giving as opposed to personal time.

In the *executive elite school,* the theme is excellence. The emphasis is on being the best. There are always discussions on the need for preparation and top quality performance. Students are expected to tow the line and be self disciplined. The academic pace in the executive elite school is accelerated. A great deal of time is devoted to building the ability of analyzing information and critical thinking. It is assumed that these young people will occupy many of the high level positions in business, government, law, medicine, science, and education.

I have had the pleasure of traveling and speaking to students and schools all across America. I can attest to the fact that rural schools and urban schools do not have the advantages of the more wealthy suburban and private schools. Essentially, there is no comparison between them when it comes to supplies, equipment, material, and technology.

Are we really under the impression that kids coming out of such different environments with such divergent expectations can realistically be held to the same expectations once they have "graduated"?

We must create a more equitable system in education in order for all children to have similar opportunities to grow and succeed.

Rise Up

Help elevate youth to a higher level of self-awareness. Provide visible examples of morality. Allow them to have an active role in making decisions that directly affect their lives.

Al Porter

CHAPTER TWO

Rise Up

Many believe that America has reached, and perhaps sur passed, the zenith of her greatness—that she is destined to become a second-rate world power. Millions more believe America is on the brink of economic collapse and moral ruin, and may lead the world into nuclear Armageddon, attempting to hold on to her position of power and prestige, according to E.G. White in his book, *Will America Survive?*

The Crisis Of Youth

Unfortunately, we are confronted with that question when we hear about children like Robert Sandifur, an 11-year-old living in Chicago. According to young people in the neighborhood, no one liked him because he was a bully. A local store owner called him a "crooked son-of-a-bitch." While shooting at a group of rival gang members, he shot and killed a 14-year-old girl. He quickly became a liability to the gang who put him up to it. The gang found two brothers who happened to be honor students and wanted to be in their gang. The gang instructed them to kill the 11 year old. Authorities found his body in a bloody pool of mud underneath the railway system in South Chicago. He had been shot gangland-style in the back of the head.

Although the social service agencies knew about him, they failed in preventing a horrible tragedy. They knew that he was born to a teenage crack addict and his father was a criminal. He circulated between foster homes, detention centers, and safe houses. Despite multiple arrests, he was ordered by Illinois law to be placed on probation. His Guardian, Ad Litem (public lawyer), said that Robert had been turned into a sociopath by the time he was 3-years-old.

Our juvenile justice system was designed in the Nineteenth Century. Young people didn't commit felony crimes; certainly not at the rate they do today. We could send them home and almost be assured that the parents would handle the problem. But in 1996, we know that many of the parents are sociopaths themselves. And perhaps we should remove the child until we can get some help for the parents.

A psychiatrist asked Robert, the 11-year-old, to complete the sentence, "I am very . . .". "Sick," Robert said. The doctor said that he was full of self hate, lonely, illiterate, and wary. His mother had been arrested 41 times for prostitution. He was being raised by his grandmother who was described as having a "severe borderline personality disorder." He never stood a chance!! It is the responsibility of those who have children to make every effort to bring to fruition, at the very least, a stable adult.

I hope that, as adults, we are not under the impression that this is an isolated incident. Children are fighting back the only way they know how. The Menendez brothers were from a wealthy family and had it all. Or so we thought! Their troubles were as a result of adult problems. Amy Fisher grew in a nice New York neighborhood and her troubles were as a result of adult problems. It is not only an inner-city phenomena. Problems from teen pregnancy to dropping out of school can, in many cases, be traced to an adult influence.

It is not only the fact that many adults behave irresponsibly; many make a great living exploiting teens. The teen market is worth 115 billion dollars per year. Obviously someone must sell sneakers worth $150. Everything from hair mousse to Dockers to new cars to daytime talk shows seek to impact this lucrative target audience.

We know how much money our children spend per year, but we don't know how to encourage them to excel and to feel better about themselves. We must Rise Up!

Morality vs. Entertainment

We may very well have reached that place of moral ruin when our television sets broadcast more than 6,000 hours a year of talk shows which exploit guests for the amusement of the audience. We watch as people are embarrassed and humiliated every day on national television. Topics like "My mother is sleeping with my boy friend", "Help, my son is a Drag Queen!", or "One Night Stand Re-Unions" are pretty much common, so much so, that these titles are quite tame by comparison.

It has gotten so bad that we have even stopped asking whether the behavior is right or wrong. We push the envelope of decency all under the guise of entertainment. The fact that an 18-year-old woman just admitted that she likes to get stuporously drunk, get behind the wheel of a car, and go from bar to bar to pick up men with the purpose of having sex should really worry most of the people in the audience and at home, but it doesn't. The people hoot, holler, and scream for more. No one was concerned that the young man sitting on stage in a full length gown, six inch Stiletto heels, enough make-up to make even Michael Jackson envious, nails, and hair down his back obviously needed someone to talk to. Instead, the audience requested that he perform a Diana Ross number.

We hunger to be shocked and surprised. A live confrontation between two women over some cheating man is enough to make us salivate. We drag out moms who dress too sexy and they, the parents, get on stage and parade around in front of screaming and barking men, as their daughters shrink in humiliation, begging their mothers to cover up. We can't turn it off when a young woman with five nose rings, who confesses to being in a gang, tells the audience how many men she has beaten up and robbed. Members of the audience cheer as she even threatens them **personally**!

The more we continue to put this kind of programming in front of young people, the worse it will become. How far does the envelope have to be pushed before we realize the devastating impact our lack of guidance has had and continues to have. The implications are potentially disastrous. Our youth are becoming almost immune to the pain of others which makes it easier to disobey parents, disrespect teachers, beat up girlfriends, rob, steal, or kill.

The Ultimate Fighting Challenge pits "Warriors" against each other in a battle to the finish, until one of the men is physically unable to continue. And we love it!! We want blood, gore, and faces beaten to a bloody pulp. And we will pay handsomely to buy the show on cable television. How far can we possibly be from televising "**fights to the death!**"

An MTV show entitled, Singled Out, gathers 50 young, attractive women and one "stud" for whom the women are to compete through a series of questions from categories such as breast size, legs, experience, hair, height, and weight. The crowd is finally whittled down to the winner. On the other side, men are categorized by their car, job, apartment, money, and physique.

Much like the cultural revolution of the 1960's, this generation is seeking to find its place in the world. But unlike the parents of the 1960's, we have failed as adults to responsibly monitor what is offered to our children. We are allowing them to grow under the impression that this is all just normal fun. We can't stop the shows from being televised but we can control, to some extent, what is seen in our own homes.

Adultism

Young people are suffering from adultism. Just like the sexism and racism that we grew up fighting, there is yet another "ism" to be concerned about. Adultism is simple. Adults have the power and teens don't!

We have to realize that our children know about the way people behaved in the 1960's and 70's. Love was free and drugs were plenty, and many people indulged with reckless abandon. They learned these things through the very medium through which they watch Ricki Lake, Sally, and Montel. We are not in a position of great morality when we say "Just Say No!" Someone has to set some examples. It is foolish to say, "do what I say and not as I do", keep a straight face, and not feel like a complete hypocrite. It is more reasonable to tell young people the dangers of drugs, alcohol, and sex too early, than to come from a moral, "holier than thou" vantage point, which many of us can't claim anyway.

How can we explain that we, as a generation inherited, wealth and abundance (we mean America as a whole), and now we hand over to them debt, poverty, despair, and uncertainty. All this while blaming them for it.

Let's face it, the figures are getting worse. Last year our teenagers killed more than 3,000 people, they raped more than 5,000, robbed 30,000, and assaulted nearly 67,000 people. We look at those figures and think, "WOW, what is happening", and shake our heads in disgust.

However, in the same time period, this very age group were the victims of 358,000 cases of neglect, 205,000 cases of physical abuse, 127,000 cases of sexual abuse, and 108,000 cases of emotional maltreatment. All at the hands of adults. It would appear as though they are just fighting back! Their outrageous behavior is a direct result of our outrageous behavior.

The Tufts University Center for Hunger, Poverty, and Nutrition estimated that 30 million American children went hungry in 1992. That represented an increase of 50 percent since the mid-1980's.

Why do young people do poorly in school? Why do young people do drugs, or hang out on street corners, or get pregnant? A common answer to those questions is that many teens have low self-esteem. This is a poor sense of one's own self worth or ability; a lack of confidence. Professional literature about adolescents, social service priorities, and funding trends emphasize programs which build self-esteem.

When we think back to our adolescent years, we begin to notice how much we wanted to do and how little power we had to do it. We wanted to go places that we couldn't. We wanted to try to do things we were not supposed to. We wanted to affect and change classes at school, our community, and our neighborhood, and weren't able to. We never had the money, wheels, friends, influence, or credibility to make a difference.

There were lots of promises from adults. If I study hard, stay out of fights, stay safe, don't have sex, don't drink or smoke, or don't mess up, adults promised us a life filled with power and privileges. For many of us who follow that advice, we have the expectation that things are going to naturally fall into place because we feel that we have upheld some sacred order of youth; and that was to follow adult's advice. However, when we stepped out to finally claim our prize at the end of this faith-filled journey, we discovered that for the most part it was a blatant lie. O.K., I was naive for believing it, but who knew?

Power

Another major contributor to the problems young people have is a lack of power. They have no power over their own lives. Without power to protect themselves, they are constantly restricted, disrespected, and abused by us. At home, at school, at work, in the streets--adults have the authority to decide how they should dress, how they should talk, where they can and cannot be, and who they can be there with. We decide their future through discipline, records, arrests, report cards, evaluations, allowances, and/or the lack or neglect of all of these things.

Yet, the promise of better things to come if they just behave themselves, in reality, is merely an empty promise. The thing we adults don't realize is that our young people know that the promise is mostly a lie. We are only fooling ourselves.

Well, what can our kids really expect? They can expect limited educational opportunities, unemployment, unplanned families, dysfunctional relationships, and an epidemic of violence.

But we still turn around and blame them for our failure. We label teens as being irresponsible, trouble makers, immature, apathetic, lazy, dishonest, underachievers, and stupid. We define this failure as a personal problem for each teen, a failure of self-esteem, and teens end up blaming themselves or attacking each other. The violence we see involving teen-to-teen abuse that happens in gangs, in couples, or from the school bully or the self abuse from drugs and alcohol, unwanted pregnancy and suicide can be seen as a form of learned helplessness, hopelessness, and lovelessness in teens. Dr. Cornell West calls this condition nihilism. Life without meaning, hope, and love breeds a cold-hearted, mean-spirited outlook that can destroy any individual.

As long as teens are looked upon as "them" by adults, they will forever shoulder the burden of doing all the work necessary in convincing adults that they are actually worthy of respect. What we must realize is that people, especially degraded and oppressed people like teen-agers, are hungry for identity, meaning, and self-worth. We need to rise up and lift ourselves above our own self-important attitudes and realize how badly we are hurting our young people. Teens need strong and powerful allies who can shift the emphasis from raising their self-esteem to increasing their power. This will allow the exuberance, insight, and creativity of young people to contribute to the betterment of all of us.

Listen Up

Counter every negative report about teens with something positive. For each negative action by a teenager, there are at least 50-100 positive acts that go totally uncovered. Curtail the mixed messages that we adults send. "Do as I say and not as I do!"

Al Porter

—Chapter Three—

Listen Up

We have to be concerned about the things our young people are hearing about themselves. Those of us with a legitimate desire to see young people empowered are horrified at the types of messages being sent to them by the very people who, again, want to bargain with them. If you do "this" then "that" will be forthcoming. This is the same lie they told me and even perhaps told you.

It Ain't My Fault

We adults have become quite gifted at the "blame game." For instance, I've heard teens being told by someone who I used to respect, that they were to blame for the dismal performance of American teens when pitted against other teens from the world's industrialized countries. "We're in last place and it's all your fault," they said. She continued to rail on with examples of poor performance by American teen-agers.

And while much of her information was correct, she did not stop to say anything positive about them. It is true that a few years ago American youth finished dead last in math and next to last in science when they competed against the top 20 countries in the world. And what did we do, but make them feel even worse by making them feel as though it was all their fault.

When we snap out of our blaming mode, we must grapple with the fact that kids don't run the school districts, they don't teach the classes, they don't design the curriculum, train people in instructional methodologies, or place levies on the ballot to secure additional funding for new equipment, materials, and supplies. Teenagers don't have a hand in the running of the school district whatsoever. How then can we burden them with the blame for our failure to teach them? It is not their failure, it's our failure: teachers, parents, and school district officials.

Diane Ravitch called this generation of young people numb as in "numskull," dumb, academically inept, and a waste of time. She suggested that we basically give up and focus more attention on the next generation. Who, I wonder, does Ms. Ravitch think will be raising this next generation? It would matter very little what we do in school or how great our programs are if the next generation has to go home to dumb, numb, academically inept parents.

We have provided enough evidence to suggest to these young people that we could not care less about them. Both our words and our deeds have suggested it. Why then, should they care about anything we have to say to them. It is obvious they have, in essence, cast a vote of "no confidence". Ask yourself, honestly, how you would feel if you were a teenager today? And what possible incentives do we give except empty promises of success 20 years from now?

Bad News

Today the headlines in our local paper read "Gang Violence Overtaking Local School". There is a propensity to broadcast what's wrong instead of what's right! There were probably 100 positive things going on in the school, but our glorification of the negative would never allow us to report it. Its everywhere! "The Schools Are Plagued With Violence", "Teachers Are Afraid of The Students", "Test Scores At All Time Low", "Drop Out Rate At All Time High" are typical headlines that many of us see so much that we have become oblivious to them.

Well, what about the good news? Why are there so few good news stories depicting teens in the many positive roles they play in society? After all, it is just a small minority of youth who cause most of the problems. Although the small minority is larger than the small minority was when I was growing up, the overwhelming majority of young people are positive.

We must adopt the philosophy of making sure that the good news regarding young people and their progress gets told. Nobody has bothered to mention that there are more than seven times the number of geniuses in this current generation than in their grandparents' generation. Nobody ever says that there seventeen times the number of people who could be considered gifted and talented than in their grandparents' generation. These numbers, of course, are relative. If these children were in 1950, most of them would be geniuses or classified as gifted and talented. It would help if we said something about the fact that 88 percent of all teens have a positive outlook on the future. That more than 50 percent of them are active volunteers, that 75 percent of them have above average friendship making skills, and 86 percent have what could be considered very high educational goals.

But against this, we have only 26 percent of parents having any kind of role whatsoever in the school, only 48 percent of teens enjoy good parental communication and a meager 39 percent of them have communication with any other adult.

When Ravitch called them dumb and numb, she should also talk about the fact that last year a group of American teenagers walked away with the Gold Medal at the Science and Math Olympics in China. But what was so great beyond that is that they ALL made perfect scores! And at the same time made history for being the first group to do that in the 45 year history of the Science and Math Olympics. But did any one hear about it? Probably a small percentage of us noticed the small blip about it in *Time* magazine. They didn't even devote enough space to the story to have room to mention the names of the seven young people.

Wait a minute!! These young people have made a tremendous accomplishment. They have restored our national academic pride! We could use this information to motivate children by demonstrating the possibilities. We could inspire teachers who have become frustrated and need an infusion of positive news about the profession.

If they had gone over and finished last again, where do you think the story would have been? You guessed it, Page One!

I worked for a while for a newspaper as a writer. I covered school districts as part of my job. I would often find something happening in the schools that would depict the positives. I wanted to cover the good news and was told that good news stories are "fluff", and that it was not really considered real news because it did not interest the entire community.

How can kids have high levels of self-esteem if we hide most of the positive news from them? A major role for school districts today is to continue to feed the positives to their community regarding the school district and student successes.

Parents need to take more of an active role in their children's education. That does not mean volunteering in the school, necessarily, but it does mean picking up the report card personally, at least meeting the teachers, and, occasionally, if not everyday, picking them up from school.

X Generation

How would you feel if you were called an X? Malcolm X replaced his American last name with an X because he did not know what his original heritage was. He did not know his real identity so he placed the X there to denote the fact that he simply did not know. When we are told by our algebra teachers to solve for X, it also represents the unknown, a mystery that we need to uncover. When we call this generation of young people "Generation X", we are in essence telling them that we don't know them and we don't know what the future holds for them.

Unfortunately, these little cute names seem to stick. Baby-boomers are now in the White House! The label will last an entire lifetime. What we need to tell them is that the X stands for the fact that it represents a need to ***examine*** the situation of negativity, to ***exercise*** good judgment because there is a need for them to serve as an ***example*** of what is possible, and yield to the ***expectation*** that they do their best while going the ***extra*** mile in order to ***excel*** in everything they do. And if we are going to accept an X as a label, then it should stand for ***excellence***!!

When you hear someone refer to this generation as an X, simply respond:

The X Stands for Excellence!

We must begin to infuse more positives about teens. All mediums are available from radio to television to print to on-line. Federal regulations require that radio and television stations devote a specified number of hours to public affairs programming. We, as educators and parents, must begin to tell the good stories. Messages come in all forms, but no form makes a greater impact on youth than music.

Musical Messages

We just went through an era of what was called "Gangsta" rap. This musical form evolved from the rap music of the late 1970's. It was a much different art form at that time. For the most part, people were still singing about love, cheating, heartbreak, and romance, so this new thing called rap was a great diversion. The first one I can recall was "Rapper's Delight" by The Sugarhill Gang.

I was about 17 and had a job at a restaurant in a suburban St. Louis Mall. I had to ride the bus to get there. The bus ride was two hours. My brother Richard, who was 19 at the time, also worked at the restaurant. Obviously he had gotten a copy of the "album" and he memorized the entire sixteen minutes of the rap. He did that rap unrelentlessly for the entire bus ride both to and from work. It drove me absolutely nuts!! The lyrics for part of the rap when like this: "I said a hip-hop a hebit to the hip-hip-hop you don't stop a rocking to the bang-bang boogie say up jump the boggie to the rhythm of the boogie to beat." Or at least that's what it sounded like! So what does that mean? I had no idea what they meant. The lyrics were obviously simple and somewhat meaningless, but today, it has grown into messages like the one delivered by Public Enemy who said "Fight the Power—You got to fight the powers that be!" They never clarified for us exactly what powers we were supposed to be fighting. Many of us who are at least reasonably intelligent can, of course, distinguish fantasy from reality. But what about younger children who are quite impressionable and who look upon these particular adults as role models. The number is estimated in the millions. Don't we owe our kids more guidance? The Geto Boys said, "My mind is playing tricks on me." The reason his mind was playing tricks is because he was engaged in illegal activity, both selling and abusing drugs. Ice Cube exclaimed that "Today was a good day!" Today was a good day because he didn't have to use his "AK" (sub machine gun). Nobody in his neighborhood was killed today, so it was a good day. This says that we expect someone to die every day and we accept it as a reality. It is a reality because we allow it to be a reality.

It's not just rap music that should cause concern. Although, admittedly, I'm not a devoted Rock follower, I can say that the names of the groups alone are enough to cause great concern. For example, Mega Death, Slayer, Bio-Hazard, Suicidal Tendencies, and God Lives Underwater are a few that come to mind. Even the safe haven of Country and Western has been disturbed when Dolly Parton shouted, "I've got the PMS Blues." She said, "I've got the hair-frizzing, nail-biting, butt-kicking, man-killing, PMS Blues." Even though we think of this as cute, will little girls believe that PMS is an acceptable reason for violence?

Finding Your Power

We need to "Find our power" instead of "Fighting the power". Everyone has a power, a special talent or skill that they have a mastery for. Dr. Deepak Chopra calls this the Law of Least Effort. The Law of Least Effort is based on the fact that nature's intelligence functions with effortless ease and abandoned carefreeness. This is our natural talent. We all have it!

He says that if you observe nature at work, you will see that least effort is expended. Grass doesn't try to grow, it just grows. Fish don't try to swim, they just swim. Flowers don't try to bloom, they bloom. Birds don't try to fly, they just fly. It is the nature of the sun to shine, and it is human nature to make our dreams manifest into a physical reality with tremendous ease.

Least effort is expended when our actions are motivated by love of what we are doing. When we start seeking power and control over other people's lives, we waste energy. When we seek money or power for the sake of our egos, we spend energy chasing the illusion of happiness instead of enjoying the happiness of the moment. When we seek money for personal gain only, we cut off the flow of energy to ourselves and interfere with the expression of nature's intelligence.

According to Chopra, The Law of Least Effort has three components:

The first is ***Acceptance***—Acceptance of people, situations, circumstances and events as they occur.

The second is ***Responsibility***—Responsibility means not blaming others for your situation, including yourself. Having the ability to have a creative response to the situation as it is now. Once we do this, every so-called upsetting situation will become an opportunity for the creation of something new, and every so-called tormentor or tyrant will become your teacher. Reality is an interpretation. If you choose to interpret reality in this way, you will have many teachers around you and many opportunities to evolve.

The third is ***Defenselessness***—Which means that our awareness is established in defenselessness, and you have relinquished the need to convince or persuade others of your point of view. If we just relinquish our need to defend our points of view, we will gain access to enormous amounts of energy that have been previously wasted.

By teaching the Law of Least Effort, we can teach our young people to find their power, and maybe, some of us can even find our own.

Hurry Up

Help young people develop a sense of community and service to humanity. Helping others who are less fortunate than ourselves will reveal how much we have to be truly thankful for.

Al Porter

CHAPTER FOUR

Hurry Up

A friend came up to me and said, "Al, did you know that on the day you were born, the world was about to be blown up?" I said, "No, but thanks for sharing that bit of information. You're such an inspiration!!"

I was born in the fall of 1962. The world was poised and waiting for the blast. We were right in the middle of the Cuban Missile Crisis. President Kennedy and the United States were literally staring down the barrel of a Communist gun only 100 miles off the Florida coast. The world was about to experience its last war, if an agreement could not be reached between the United States and the Soviet Union.

Kennedy stood by his position that the missiles had to be removed or there would be a complete blockade of the Cuban Island and potentially a "full-scale attack" on the Soviet Union. Failure on Kennedy's part would have allowed nuclear missiles within a half hour striking distance to Washington D.C., not to mention the scores of other American cities all along the East coast. They would have been left wide open for missile attack.

People were beside themselves with terror. I have listened to the people who were living through it with particular interest because this was all happening just as I was making my great world entrance. People were purchasing underground bunkers and stocking up on food and the supplies they would need in case of a nuclear blast. The drills in school were the most horrifying. My oldest brother told me that they were made to hide under their desks during a drill. He laughingly asked, "what good would that have done? We did it because they told us to. We thought they knew what they were talking about."

After a great deal of tension, the Soviets pulled their missiles out of Cuba and Kennedy was able to avert World War III. I admire Kennedy for his courage and his decisiveness. In my opinion, it made him a great man!

Doing For Others

Remarkably, I don't remember Kennedy as much for that as I do for saying, "Ask not what your country can do for you, but what you can do for your country." Kennedy had a great sense of community spirit and service to humanity. He initiated the Peace Corps movement whereby

Americans went all over the world to assist disadvantaged countries in the areas of agriculture, economics, political structure, industry, and education. Kennedy saw a need to serve people who had nothing and no hope.

Ameri-Corp Program

We now have some of the very conditions present in those troubled nations right here in America. Recognizing this, much to his credit, President Clinton created the Ameri-Corp Program. The goal of the program is similar to those of the Peace Corps, to inspire young people with a spirit of caring and giving to others. The main ingredient in the program is that adults demonstrate to teens that we care about them first. Our local program in the Columbus, Ohio area is called City Year. This program has done tremendous things both for the city of Columbus and for the self-esteem of the young people in the program. Through giving, they have the opportunity to see exactly how fortunate they are themselves.

Members have the opportunity to volunteer to rebuild the communities of the inner-city, serve on neighborhood patrols against drugs and crime, assist senior citizens by helping around the house, shopping, or keeping them company, or working with the day care center as a teacher's aide. Young people are presented with a chance to do a number of very positive things through the program. On the one hand, they help out the community, and, on other hand, they build their college fund for higher education.

I've seen what the program can do. Two young men who attended the high school where I worked, participated in the program. The thing about these two young men was that if trouble were money, they would have been millionaires. They were both unceremoniously thrown out of school. The next time I saw them they were participating as a part of a group of extremely excited young people at a city ceremony. I found out that they finished GED programs and immediately enrolled in the City-Year Program, looking enthusiastically toward the future. It seems to be just the type of empowering tool we need for young people right now.

But the program has become the victim of political games. Congress, led by House Speaker Newt Gingrich, canceled the funding for the program calling it "a pork barrel project". At the same time the very same members of Congress are recommending that we give more money to military than it said it needed. Last year, the Office of Management and Budget reported $51 billion in direct subsidies to industries and another $53 billion in corporate tax breaks. This year, Congress is proposing to cut only $1.5 billion from this trove. If we took only one percent of this money, we could fund the Ameri-Corp Program nationally for almost three years.

And that's not the worst of it! There is currently a $245-billion multi-year tax break on the table for rich corporations and the well off. All this while claiming that we have no money to send poverty stricken, deserving young men and women to college who help out their communities through volunteerism. At the very least, the young people are willing to work for it!!

The sense of nihilism that Dr. West talked about means, among other things, that there is a feeling that no one really cares. Now, our kids are learning how to not care as well.

Over the years, we have lost a great deal of our desire in giving our time for other people. The latest figures show a significant decline in the number of volunteer hours among the general population. According to the United States Statistical Report, the percentage of Americans doing volunteer work has fallen to just above 50 percent.

Real Life Hero—C.D. Banks

We all come across people in our lives who seem to have a higher level of dedication and commitment. The kind of people who are able to express a perfect combination of love and discipline for you. C.D. Banks was the kind of person who truly had a dedication for youth.

C.D. Banks was a older gentleman who lived in a two room shack surrounded by vacant lots. On any given day of the week, he had an average of 100 kids in and around his house. He erected basketball hoops on the vacant lots along with horseshoe stakes and badminton and volleyball nets, and turned a field across the street into a baseball diamond. He ran all the sports leagues right from his house. He hired many of the older guys to coach and be recreational leaders, setting the examples of behavior. He had every board game imaginable. Going to his house was literally like going to fun palace. What ever you thought you wanted to do recreationally you could bet C.D. could provide the opportunity for you. His windows were filled with trophies and photographs of most of us in some type of "bigtime" sports pose trying to look like the Heisman trophy.

He did all these things for us, and many of us never even once said thank you to him. He gave unselfishly to us from his very soul. We didn't, at that time, look at him as though he was a hero because I believe that we were under the impression that he was replaceable. We thought that if it wasn't C.D., it would be someone else who would fulfill that role.

He was a hero! I never saw him mad, heard him complain, or ask for anything. That's hard to imagine when you consider that we behaved worse than Bay-Bay's kids.

One day, one of the older guys announced that C.D. was in the hospital. He didn't really know why but that he should be there for several days. It turned out that he had an infection in his foot that was gangrenous and had been neglected for quite a number of years. Doctors had to remove one of his legs up to the knee. We looked upon this as dreadful news. Not, as you would think, because we loved C.D., which we did, but rather because we thought that it would mean an end to the baseball, basketball, and football seasons that we had become accustomed to C.D. running. He had done all he could for us, and initially, we thought more about ourselves than we did about him.

One of the most important lessons he taught all of us was to be self respectful and yield respect to others regardless of who they were.

Although the methodology by which we learned to respect others and ourselves was unorthodox, it was effective. C.D. left it up to the older guys to dish out discipline. If we walked inside wearing a hat, we had to endure a few punches or for that matter, quite a few punches depending how fast we were able to remove it. We quickly learned not to wear hats indoors. If we swore we would receive the same type treatment. If we exhibited disrespectful behavior towards another member, for example pushing, shoving, fighting, and purposefully insulting, we would have much explaining to do, and it better be good.

Of course, we played the dozens. But in my old neighborhood we called it "joning". For instance, "Yo mama so dumb that she thought a quarterback was a refund", or "Yo sister so fat she wears hula-hoops to hold up her stockings", or "Yo breath is so bad that when you open your mouth trees wither". This was acceptable fun because we knew that they were just jokes. Except, every now and then, when someone really got in a good one, the other guy would want to fight, but, again, the aggression was quelled by the older members.

Discipline among the neighborhood kids, at least at C.D.'s, was not a problem. What is most amazing, however, is that if C.D. Banks were alive today and still trying to save lives, he would be in jail for child abuse!! The odd thing is that I never felt abused, I felt protected. The number of lawsuits against him would be staggering if he were alive now.

Lawsuit Mania

I hate to admit it but Dan Quayle said it first, "America has too many lawyers!" About 70 percent of the world's attorneys live right here in the United States. We began in the late 1970's with frivolous lawsuits. Everybody was suing everybody else over the most simple things, and the attitude has gotten much worse. Back then, it was Hyatt Legal Services. They were the first lawyers I remember seeing on T.V. They were nice people offering low cost legal services to people who needed representation and otherwise could not afford it. Today, we can't get away from them on television, the radio, newspapers, and even billboards. They often ask if we've been injured and need help—by the time they're through talking, not only are we convinced that our back pain is a direct result of the woman who backed into us with her cart at the supermarket three days ago, but we're ready to testify under oath that it was with malicious intent!!

Our quickness to sue our neighbors has had a negative effect on the way we look at our willingness to volunteer. Many people will not coach little league because they have been sued. Many people will not help the scouting programs because accidents have left them personally liable. The same thing has happened with volunteerism in schools. Although charitable contributions are up, time actually spent in community service is down.

We must hurry up and provide more examples of reaching out, sharing, and helping our fellow man. No matter how great or small the time commitment is, it will make a tremendous impact. Kennedy had the right idea. We must develop a sense of community spirit and service to humanity. There are thousands of programs to become involved with. Many of them need volunteers. We can make a great impact on today and tomorrow.

Cheer Up

Wishing without action creates disillusionment. Vision and action will yield success. There is no need to wish upon a star, blow out the birthday candles or rub Aladdin's lamp. Teach them that they don't need a magic genie, because they have the magic inside.

Al Porter

CHAPTER FIVE

Cheer Up

As children, we were told to wish hard for the things we wanted most. All we had to do was be **good** and the wishes would be granted. At Christmas, we were told that Santa would slide down the chimney and bestow upon all the good little boys and girls the toys they wanted most of all in the whole wide world. I was suspicious early on. Not only did we not have a chimney, but if anyone was ever caught in the projects with a great big bag of presents, he would not have gotten too far!

On our birthday we are told to blow the candles out and make a wish. When we see a shooting star we are supposed to wish upon it. When we go shopping at the Mall, we are supposed to throw coins into the fountain and wish for good luck. We rip the chicken apart to find the wish bone, snatch it in two and whoever gets the largest piece will receive a wish. We look for four leaf clovers in the field all day long so that we might be granted something. When our teeth fall out many of us were thrilled as children because we knew that the tooth fairy would be making a visit soon. We are conditioned early on to wish for the things we want. As children, it was a lot of fun.

Certainly as adults, we cannot engage in this behavior and expect to be taken seriously. Obviously, however, many of us got stuck in time. We should know by now that wishing is counterproductive. We send the listener the message that we have a losing attitude and that someone else is in control of our destiny.

We seem to have that type of wishing mentality, when it comes down to making sure that our young people have the tools they need in order to grow into responsible, productive citizens. We have this same mind set when we hope for solutions to crime, poverty, drug abuse, and illegitimacy among our children. Many of us adopt an "I wish they would do something" philosophy, wishing that the government would do something tomorrow and by the next day, poof, like magic, the problems will be solved.

Cheer up because we have the magic! Suppose we were to stop wishing and start doing. What it boils down to is this: do we have the power to effect change right now? The answer to that question is yes. We have the power to accomplish anything we truly desire.

The first thing we must do is to delete the wish from our vocabulary forever. By doing this, we decrease the likelihood that we'll engage in wishful thinking. Our attitude will naturally become one of "can-do". Stop looking at the difficulties with young people as insurmountable. Instead, begin to make smaller goals that are achievable. Break the whole dream down into smaller pieces. Instead of saying we are going to get rid of teen drinking, let's create a program which targets 13-19 year olds within our own home area. We could provide workshops, speakers, alternative activities, and conferences, and have the young people become a speaker's bureau of their own, going to elementary schools to discuss the issue. Bottom line, make sure that the goal is one that can be accomplished.

Short-Term Goals

In my favorite Charlie Brown episode, Charlie was having a pretty bad day. He had struck out for the third straight time. In frustration, he yells, "Rats!" He goes back to the dugout, buries his face in his glove, and cries to Lucy. "I'll never be a big-league player. All my life, I have dreamed of playing in the majors, but I know I'll never make it."

Lucy says, "You're thinking way too far in advance, Charlie Brown. What you need are more immediate goals."

"Immediate goals?" he asked.

"Yeah," Lucy says. "Start right now with this next inning. When you go out to pitch, see if you can walk out to the mound without falling down."

When we begin to talk about changing the behavior of our young people, we need to make sure that the goals we are making are both achievable and manageable ones.

Take Action

Winter in St. Louis provided a great deal of opportunity for my friends and I to benefit from the need adults had to stay inside where it was warm. Whenever it snowed, we would grab shovels and go in search of some poor adult who looked discouraged by nature's sense of humor. Our youthful ingenuity led us to people whose walkways or driveways were half finished. It was obvious that they had lost complete interest in the task and would usually be thrilled to turn over the work along with several dollars if we finished the work they started.

I find a lot of truth in Abraham Lincoln's statement that "All things *come to those who wait but only what's left over from those who hustle."*

A commitment to finish what we start will determine our satisfaction and success with everything we do.

I Can Do That!!

I was working in a high school in Dayton, Ohio in 1990. The school was a mixed, yet predominantly black school. I ran a career education program and seemed to have a knack for it. I loved the students. They were enthusiastic, and I fed off their positive energy. It was a great job but I knew that this was not my "power"—that skill, gift, talent, or whatever you want to call it.

I had heard of Harvey Alston, and knew that he was a professional speaker who was gaining an international reputation. He spoke for various conferences for the students and staff of our program. I begrudgingly attended a closing ceremony and he was the speaker, and I thought he was "all right". I actually laughed out loud a couple of times. I decided to see if we might get him to speak for a multicultural program at the high school where I worked.

On the day of our program, Harvey showed up early, tuxedo, bald head, bow tie, and all. The previous year, the students had practically booed and hissed the poor speaker off the platform, so naturally, the administration, who had a propensity for getting nervous before ALL school assemblies, kept asking me whether he was good.

The students spent about 45 minutes dancing, reciting, singing, and acting out dramatic skits. It was a very nice program and now it was time to introduce our speaker. I was determined to make it as hard as I possibly could for this guy. I got up and strolled casually, but at a brisk enough pace towards the microphone, trying to maintain the "cool" image that I had somehow gained. I spoke with every amount of enthusiasm and power I could muster and drew a rousing applause from the crowd. I turned the mic over to Harvey who stood totally still until every eye was on him. He glared at the audience and it fell to complete silence. "I wrote a letter to Dr. Martin Luther King Jr., and in that letter I asked him why? Why are my young black brothers killing each other? Why do we have so much hate in America? The audience was captivated as they leaned in for more. It was the first time I had really listened to him. When he finished, the students literally jumped out of their seats to award a much deserved standing ovation. I looked on in complete awe!

I told myself at that time that "I can do **that!**" I called Harvey up in Columbus and told him that I wanted to do what he was doing. He gave me unimaginable assignments. He gave me a list of ten books, told me to get them from the library, and call him back in thirty days at which time he proceeded to ask me questions regarding the reading material. I could not respond too much and while I had indeed checked the material out of the library, I had not digested enough of it in the 30 day time frame. I had to endure a two hour lecture on not being prepared. It continued that way for nearly a year. "How can you soar with eagles in the morning when you are languishing with buzzards at night?" he would ask during one of many surprise 4:00 a.m. phone calls. He almost instinctually knew that I was just getting home from the "Shake It Up, Shake It Down" Nightclub.

I had no idea at that time that Harvey Alston would become a "father-brother-friend" to me. Since that time, he has been my mentor and I have now traveled nationally speaking to young people. Harvey's message is to be the best in everything we do. My program encourages academic achievement, community service, self-awareness, rejecting negative messages and stereotypes, believing in our abilities, and having accomplishable goals.

Goals

I've dreamed many dreams that never came true,
I've seen them vanish at dawn;
But I've realized enough of my dreams, thank God,
To make me want to dream on.
I've prayed many prayers when no answer came,
I've waited patient and long;
But answers have come to enough of my prayers
To make me keep praying on.
I've trusted many a friend who failed
And left me to weep alone;
But I've found enough of my friends true-blue
To make me keep trusting on.
I've sown many seeds that fell by the way
For the birds to feed upon;
But I've held enough golden sheaves in my hand,
To make me keep sowing on.
I've drained the cup of disappointment and pain,
I've gone many days without song,
But I've sipped enough nectar from the rose of life
To make me want to live on.

Anonymous

Look Up

Help them create a vision of where they want to go in life. Tell them to reject the inclination to internalize harmful images of themselves, and not to adopt someone else's negative predictions about their potential.

Al Porter

CHAPTER SIX

Look Up

My fourth grade teacher, *the first one,* was one of the best arguments for forced retirement I've ever known. She was unrelenting in her bitterness. I had been transferred into her class from another fourth grade group where I felt liked and eager to learn.

Fourth Grade Blues

I don't remember exactly when it began, or for that matter, why, but she started calling me names like pitiful, lazy, and sad. She told me that I was destined to be a failure. She asked me questions like, "What is your problem?" and "When are you going to get it right?" I used to hate going to school because I knew that whatever I did was not going to be good enough for her.

That was the 1971-72 school year and corporal punishment, at least at my school, was still the rule. Teachers used paddles for discipline, and I most certainly did not get the short end of that stick! I was disciplined more, held in from recess more, and criticized more than any other child in the group. I was horrified of her!

She actually indicated that I might wind up in jail because of my disruptive behavior. I thought that I was pretty tame compared to my friends, Michael Yancey and Antoine Gamble, who were the real cut-ups in class.

In the fourth grade, I thought teachers knew everything. There had never been a question that I had asked up through that point that my teacher could not answer or at least comment on. So, when my teacher expressed such little faith in my abilities, I believed what she said.

A number of problems began to manifest. I could care less about school, grades and report cards meant nothing, trying hard meant nothing, and getting to school on time meant nothing. Achievement, what was that and who cared anyway? I began to act in the ways in which she described me—lazy, sad, and pitiful. I had internalized what she had said and now believed it. Marcus Aurelius once said: *Your life is an expression of all your thoughts* .

She not only held me back in the fourth grade, but to add further insult, I was shipped off to another school. Do you know what it feels like to have an entire school give up on you? I do, and so do many of our kids today!! Particularly the ones who always seem to be in trouble. Their self-image is in the pits.

My self-image was also until I remembered what another teacher used to tell me. She would tell me that I was "solid-gold, diamond-eyed, sapphire-dipped and silver- tipped!" Actually, Mrs. Lancaster was the other fourth grade teacher whose class I had been taken out of when they placed me in the classroom from "hell". She was a bright and cheerful woman whose personality and smile made us feel loved and cared for. We need about a million more of her today.

Five Times As Much

It is estimated that our young people hear five times as many bad messages about themselves than good ones. Is it any wonder why so many have low self-esteem? Regardless as to whether we in schools build them up, they are likely to be torn down when they get home or when many of them associate with their own peer group.

By the time we come along to validate a young person's success, they are, more than likely, so far down on themselves that the praise only provides a fleeting moment of high self-esteem. Within moments, they are almost back to where they were, self-perceptually, before our "Johnny-come-lately" compliments.

What we must teach them is that they must have their own vision of where they want to go in life. Teach them to look beyond the things that negative people around them may forecast about their lives.

All kids were not meant to be superstars in math and science. They were not meant to run 100 meters in ten seconds, nor were they all meant to be mechanically gifted. The word education derived from the Latin word "educo" which means to draw out. Our main responsibility here is to draw out the special skills our children possess. Help them identify what they can do as opposed to what they can't do.

My brother is a mechanical genius, but the St. Louis schools failed him miserably. Instead of concentrating on building his particular skills, they spent way too much time classifying, evaluating, and categorizing him into various special programs questioning why he was not reading or writing at a certain level. It was quite simple. Stop taking him out of class to run stereotypical examinations!! If they had spent as much time teaching as they did analyzing, he would have been reading and writing at the correct level.

In my years working with schools, I have seen students who have been classified as "LD" (learning disabled), and "SBH" (severe behavioral handicapped), go out and enjoy a great deal more success than the "normal" kids.

In my position as a placement counselor for high school seniors, those students who had been labeled, categorized, and made to feel that they couldn't succeed, went into the work force determined not to fail. The students who were expected to do well had difficulty in finding jobs.

The lesson they taught me is that you must want success. They also taught me to never accept someone else's labels and predictions about what I am capable of accomplishing.

The Ten Commandments Of Success

1. ***Work hard***—It is the best investment you can make.
2. ***Study hard***—Knowledge allows us to work more intelligently.
3. ***Have initiative***—Waiting to be told to do something is not an original idea.
4. ***Love what you do***—Then you will find pleasure in mastering it.
5. ***Be Exact***—Poor work will yield poor results.
6. ***Have the spirit of conquest***—You will need it to battle or overcome difficulty.
7. ***Cultivate your personality***—Personality is the key ingredient in interpersonal relations.
8. ***Help others***—The test of greatness lies in providing opportunity for others.
9. ***Be righteous***—Without morals you cannot be a leader of people.
10. ***Do your best***—If you've done your best, you've done all you can.

What Is Success?

To laugh often and love much;
To win the respect of intelligent persons
and the affection of children;
To earn the approval of honest critics
and endure the betrayal of false friends;
To appreciate beauty;
To find the best in others;
To give of one's self without the
slightest thought of return;
To accomplish a task, whether
by a healthy child, a rescued soul, a
garden patch, or a redeemed social condition;
To have played and laughed with
enthusiasm and sung with exaltation;
To know that even one life has breathed
easier because I have lived;
This is to have succeeded.

Belief

When you believe something, you accept it as real or true. When we ask young people to believe in their abilities, we are just telling them to accept their skills as being real. Once we believe that something is true, we then act as though it is.

Many kids believe that they cannot achieve, others believe no one cares, some believe that they must join gangs in order to be protected, some believe that they must act out in order to get attention, and so on. What kids believe is "real" is in fact "real" to them. Santa and the Tooth Fairy, on one hand, and survival of the fittest, on the other.

A large part of the reason why many young people commit crimes and engage in negative activities is because they believe that this will give them power and control, something that they lack, and it will also gain them notoriety.

What they all need to believe is that they can all succeed despite the circumstances of their background. That message must come mostly from parents.

They need to know and believe that perseverance and determination are among the most useful tools. President Calvin Coolidge said, "Nothing in the world can take the place of persistence. Talent will not; nothing is more common than unsuccessful people with talent. Genius will not; unrewarded genius is almost a proverb. Education will not; the world is full of educated derelicts. Persistence and determination alone are omnipotent."

We must teach them to have the same level of belief in themselves that bungee jumpers have in the elastic cord. They must really have a great amount of belief that the cord will not break. Without this level of belief, not many people would jump head first from 100 feet with nothing to break their fall but concrete. If our young people had that kind of faith in themselves, not much could stop them from becoming successful.

Never Give Up

Lay a foundation for the belief that we must all peacefully co-exist. Realize that we perpetuate untruths about people who are different from ourselves. In most cases kids are introduced to these stereotypes and attitudes at home.

Al Porter

—CHAPTER SEVEN—

Never Give Up

Dr. King asked his, now famous, question, "How Long?" and made it rhetorical by answering for himself saying, "Not Long." How long? Not Long! When the reverend posed that query, he was asking how long it would take in order for Americans to get along and move in one direction as one nation, indivisible.

Dr. King had faith that certainly by now, the year 1996, we all would have moved past where we were when he asked the question, but we, in many instances, are not. The O.J. Simpson verdict, Susan Smith, the rape in Okinawa, Japan, Proposition 187 in California, and the Million Man March has uncovered the cancerous conditions of race relations in America. I would have to answer Dr. King's question and say, "How long? **Too** Long!"

E.G. White's question is daunting, "Will America survive?" It is hard to believe that it will if we continue to move in the direction we have chosen. How long? Too long. Last week a black couple were gunned down in the Carolinas in a horrifying display of "old school" racism. What is so absolutely compelling is that the extremist individuals who committed the murders were members of the United States Army. The very people in whom we have placed our faith to go all over the world and rescue people from starvation in

Somalia and from war in Bosnia. The people we would call on to protect us, are the ones who many of us cannot trust. The leading suspects in America's most terrifying nightmare, the Oklahoma City bombing, were members of the military service who took an oath of office swearing to uphold the Constitution.

Of course, this is not meant to be some sort of indictment against any branch of the military service, but it should raise very interesting questions about where we are now and where we are heading as a nation. Our military is the finest in the world and doesn't deserve much of the negative press they receive. Over the past 50 years, they have directly fed, clothed, and protected the world. Nevertheless, the excellent training provided by our military can also be used for other purposes later in the lives of many soldiers, as we have witnessed.

Hate Groups

In 1996, there are currently more than 200 different hate groups in America. In 1995, they committed about 6,000 separate hate crimes. That is 16 of these types of crimes every single day. 16 times a day in America people are assaulted, raped, killed, or harassed because of their color, ethnicity, religious beliefs, or sexual orientation. These individuals believe that we can somehow be categorized in grades of humanity.

Grades of Humanity

Never give up on the belief that it is possible for all of us to exist together peacefully. The overwhelming majority of us have, and will continue to, live with some outward extension of good faith toward our neighbors.

It is as if some of us believe that there are grades of humanity—that somehow some of us are grade one humans, some are grade two and even grade level three human beings. We use intelligence, environment, and race to classify people. In their book, The Bell Cur*ve*, Murray and Hernstein represented that heredity plays a greater role than environment in predicting whether children will become successful adults. They continue to advance the idea that blacks are intellectually inferior based on the inferiority of their ancestry and not on the inferior environment in which most of us are reared. I would question where these gentlemen would be today if they had to live and grow up in East St. Louis! If they or their children could make it through that, and still have a positive outlook, then their argument might be a little more convincing.

Home Talk

When we are growing up, our whole world revolves around our realities; parents, community, and friends. The ideas that we hear, those who are closest to us sharing with one another as we go through our formative years, become the ideas that we bring forth in our attitudes.

According to Dr. Jawanza Kunjufu, a child's belief system, self-esteem, and sense of purpose is directly related to those of the parent. Children want to be like their parents. When they hear racial slurs, negative stereotypes and put downs flowing freely from the lips of those they admire, they assume that this is the type of behavior expected of them. At the very least, they believe it is acceptable.

The reason we have racial division is because we perpetuate it. We teach it to our children and they teach it to theirs. These lessons are taught in a large percentage of American homes. And nearly all racial and ethnic groups participate. As we search for our own uniqueness among the people of the world, we begin to point out the small differences that we have. But that is not the problem. The problem is that we then begin to point out perceived negatives about others. For example, all blacks are violent, all whites are guilty, Middle Easterners are all terrorists, Hispanics are all illegal aliens, Asians all look alike, Native Americans are all drunk, all Jews are greedy, and so on.

Not only are these messages perpetuated at home, but they are re-enforced through the media. Television programs routinely characterize groups according to our "widely" held views of each other. We can even get on national television and demonstrate to our kids that it's all right to hate. The *Geraldo Rivera Show* became infamous for its show on "Skin Heads." Roy Innis, a black activist, had his hands around the neck of a young Skin Head when chairs began to fly. There was total chaos in the studio. Geraldo suffered a broken nose when a chair landed squarely in his face. The news picked up on the story and had a field day.

We must stop teaching racist lessons to our children through our own negative behaviors and attitudes. The ideology that we espouse today will become their ideology tomorrow.

Blatant Hypocrisy

There are several times during any given year that everyone seems to get along well. In times of disaster, we toss away our supposed hatred and focus on a new nemesis. When there is an earthquake in California, we want to help the people who are suffering, regardless of color. When the Mid-West experienced record flooding, we sent money, prayers, and re-assured them that we were behind them. Color was not mentioned once. When the massive hurricane, mostly recently "Andrew", hit the southeast, the question was, "Does FEMA (Federal Emergency Management Agency) need assistance?" When President Bush told us that more than 400,000 American soldiers were off to fight in Operation Desert Storm, we were unified in our resolve that Saddam had to go. Just last night on the "48 Hours" program with Dan Rather, families of soldiers form Fort Benning, Georgia, were gathered together, crying, praying, hugging, and leaning on each other. They were soldiers' families. They weren't white soldiers' families or black soldiers' families, but they were all the same. But after every disaster has been quelled, we go back to our old, hateful ways. These hypocritical examples must stop NOW!

The saddest part of the whole thing is that most of us don't even know why we hate. We just do! Can we really claim to be intelligent people if we can dislike others through generalities? Can we really believe that all of one group of people fit into one mold and all of another group fit into another mold? The answer to those questions is no! There are liars, thieves, rapists, bank robbers, arsonists, child molesters, murderers, and psycho-paths in every race and ethnic group. So why do we hate?

I typically asked my classes who has done the most personal harm to them, someone in their racial group or someone outside their racial group? 100 percent responded that the person who has done the most harm to them looked like them. Although this sampling is far from scientific, it does illustrate the fact that we have been convinced that someone else is the Boogie Man, when in fact the Boogie Man is looking us straight in the face every time we step in front of the mirror!!

Many of our problems with race can be overcome. Once we accept that the problems are stemming from fear and ignorance, we can move toward some common sense solutions. We can begin to educate our young people to be more respectful of themselves and others.

Showing Them How

Communicating values has never been more important than it is today. The good news is, it all begins and ends with us. When it is all said and done, parents have far more influence over instilling values in their children than any other factor.

We need to remember that we pass our values on and should keep the following in mind:

1. Children get their sense of what's right and wrong from the people they love and respect, parents! No one has more influence over teaching values than you do. Your input makes all the difference.
2. When it comes to teaching values, actions speak louder than words. Young people need to see the values lived out by you. Young people have always had a "show me" attitude. Respect for life, respect for other people, honesty, integrity . . . we got these things, or lack of them, from watching our parents.
3. Families are still the best vehicle for raising children. A loving, nurturing family creates the kind of environment where they can learn right from wrong, and how to love themselves too.
4. Always take time to sit and talk, but let your children do most of the talking. Beware of the "Parent Trap" or always relating our experiences to what the child is going through. We talk so much, we bore the child, and never get to what was really bothering him/her in the first place. Listen!

What Do People Want?

According to Workforce *America Magazine*, our diverse population has different needs that we should all pay close attention to if we want to grow together and prosper.

Young people want:

✗ credit for their life experiences.

✗ to be taken seriously.

✗ to be challenged by adults and not patronized.

Women want:

✗ To be recognized as equal partners.

✗ Active support from men.

✗ Organizations and the business community to address family issues.

Men want:

✗ The same freedom to grow and express ourselves as women.

✗ To be perceived as allies and not as the enemy.

✗ To bridge the gap between dealing with women at home and at work.

People of color want:

✗ To be valued as unique individuals, as members of ethnically diverse groups, as people of different races, and as equal contributors.

✗ To establish more open, honest working relationships with people of other races and ethnic groups.

✗ The active support of white people in fighting racism and colorism.

White people want:

✗ To have their ethnicity acknowledged.

✗ To reduce the discomfort, confusion and dishonesty in dealing with people of color.

✗ To build relationships with people of color based on common goals, concerns and mutual respect for differences.

Disabled (differently abled) people want:

- ✗ Greater acknowledgment for the things that they can do as opposed to the things the can't do.
- ✗ To be challenged by peers and colleagues.
- ✗ To be included and not isolated.

Gay men and lesbians want:

- ✗ Recognition as whole human beings and not being relegated to just sexual beings.
- ✗ Equal employment protection just like all other groups.
- ✗ Increased awareness among straight people regarding the impact of homophobic behaviors in the workplace.

It can all be summed up in one word—**respect!**

Passing the Baton

For generations, Americans could look to the future and feel as though they would do better economically than their parents and that the opportunities to move ahead would always be there. A strange phenomena has occurred. Young people today are not filled with the same feelings of assuredness as were the generation directly preceding them. The Baby Boomers, who are now in the White House and in powerful positions all over the country from Corporate CEO's, school district superintendents, association executives, editors of newspapers, and executive producers of most of what we see on television, are having the time of their lives. Their dreams have come true. But what about the rest of us? I am not a member of the so called X'ers. I'm too old! But I'm too young to be a Boomer. For those of us born between 1960 and 1970, we have no particular generational title to claim. We've been called Baby Busters. We were born in a time when women began to desire more out of life than being an educated domestic. As a result, less babies were born and more women began to appear in college classrooms and in personnel offices applying for jobs. Nevertheless, we "Busters" still have the feeling that our futures can be bright. Not that they will be, but the possibility is present.

In the race for prosperity, America was way out front. We passed the baton of leadership on to each successive generation. And that generation would take us even farther ahead. When we tried to pass the baton on to this current generation, the baton was dropped and the next thing we know, we are merging with Canada and Mexico in order to sustain our standard of living. We are in a position where we need more people to buy and consume the relatively few products still manufactured in America in order to remain where we are today.

We must encourage youth today to pick up the baton and finish the race. We can still be first if we work harder to make sure that these so called X'ers have the tools they need to compete. We need to demonstrate faith in their abilities.

We must stop perpetuating divisions between our people because the simple fact is that we don't have anyone to waste. We need all of our young people to be encouraged, enlightened, enthusiastic, and empowered. We can no longer elect to throw away children like the ones in East St. Louis. Those that we express little love for will turn into the ones we fear most.

These problems can be overcome if we adopt a Never Give Up attitude. Never give up teaching the virtues of other people, never give up encouraging young people, and never give up the feeling that all of our futures, including the kids who will lead us into the new Millennium, can and will be as bright as they want to be.

The Code of Perseverance

1. I will never give up.
2. I believe that things will work out if I just hold on.
3. I will be courageous and unswayed in the face of the odds.
4. I will not allow anyone to intimidate me or deter me from my goals.
5. I will fight to overcome any physical handicaps and setbacks.
6. I will try again, and again, and yet again to accomplish what I desire.
7. I will take new faith in the knowledge that all successful people might fight defeat and adversity.
8. I will never surrender to discouragement or despair.

Herman Sherman

References

Anyon, J., *Social Class and School Knowledge*, Curriculum Inquiry, 1981.

Chopra, D., *The Seven Spiritual Laws of Success*, Amber Allen Publishing, 1994, pgs. 53-60.

Creighton, A., *Helping Teens Stop Violence*, Hunter House, 1992, pgs. 54-61.

Gibbs, N., *Murder in Miniature*, Time Magazine, 11/94, pgs. 54-59.

Kozol, J., *Savage Inequalities*, Harper Perennial, 1991, pgs 7-36.

Kunjufu, J., *Developing Positive Self Images*, African American Images, Chicago, 1984, Pg. 9.

McGeady, R., *Does God Still Love Me?*, Covenant House, 1995, Pg. 106.

EN Today,, No. 3, 10/95, Pgs. 8-9, 25 & 27.

United States Statistical Report, 1993.

Van Echelon, G., *The Speakers' Source book*, Pr entice Hall, NJ., 1988. Pgs. 184, 187, 354, 356, 373.

West, C., *Race Matters*, Beacon Press, Boston, 1993. Pgs. 13-14.

White, E.G., *Will America Survive?*, Inspiration Books East, Inc., 1988.

Winfrey, O., *What We Can All Do To Change TV.*, TV. Guide, 11/5/95, pgs. 12-18.